a pocketful of
RHYME
Imagination for a new generation

2006 Poetry Competition for 7-11 year-olds

Young**Writers**

Heart Of England Vol I
Edited by Angela Fairbrace

 Young**Writers**

First published in Great Britain in 2006 by:
Young Writers
Remus House
Coltsfoot Drive
Peterborough
PE2 9JX
Telephone: 01733 890066
Website: www.youngwriters.co.uk

SB ISBN 1 84602 640 7

Foreword

Young Writers was established in 1991 and has been passionately devoted to the promotion of reading and writing in children and young adults ever since. The quest continues today. Young Writers remains as committed to the nurturing of poetic and literary talent as ever.

This year's Young Writers competition has proven as vibrant and dynamic as ever and we are delighted to present a showcase of the best poetry from across the UK and in some cases overseas. Each poem has been selected from a wealth of *A Pocketful Of Rhyme* entries before ultimately being published in this, our fourteenth primary school poetry series.

Once again, we have been supremely impressed by the overall quality of the entries we have received. The imagination, energy and creativity which has gone into each young writer's entry made choosing the poems a challenging and often difficult but ultimately hugely rewarding task - the general high standard of the work submitted ensured this opportunity to bring their poetry to a larger appreciative audience.

We sincerely hope you are pleased with this final collection and that you will enjoy *A Pocketful Of Rhyme Heart Of England Vol I* for many years to come.

Contents

Castlefields Primary School, Bridgnorth

Amelia Holland (11)	34
Amy-Mae Brown (10)	35
Michele Chan (10)	36
Josh Savage (11)	37
Amy Corfield (10)	38
Katrina Cheshire (11)	39
Alice Wills (10)	40
Abi Freathy (11)	41
Rebekah Mondon (11)	42
Harriet May Bratt (11)	43
Emily Tennant (11)	44
Cathy Slarke (11)	45
Amy Leanne Barber (11)	46
Ollie Milligan (11)	47
Zak Chambers (11)	48
Ben Haddon (11)	49
Elliot Paulsen-Rakic (11)	50
Jack Willett (10)	51

Cheswardine Primary School, Market Drayton

Matthew McLoughlin (11)	52
Victoria Tomkinson (11)	53
Sam Emmott (11)	54
Ellenor Jane Richards (11)	55
Charlotte Johnson (11)	56
Kelly Watling (10)	57
Kate Smith (10)	58
Amy Woodcock (10)	59
Paige Wood (10)	60
Sophie Jenkins (10)	61
Alister Munro (11)	62
Jessica Evans (10)	63
Molly Jensen (10)	64
Emma Jones (10)	65

Edith Weston Primary School, Oakham

Rebecca Bailey (10)	66
Grace Hodge (11)	67
Rosie Pitts (11)	68
Keiran Carty (11)	69

Ellesmere Primary School, Ellesmere

Hadnall CE Primary School, Shrewsbury

Luke Williams (9)   148
Conor Johnson (9)   149

Ordsall Primary School, Retford
Charlie Warren (8)   150
Megan Lyth (8)   151
Joanna Allman (9)   152

Pontesbury CE Primary School, Shrewsbury
Kestra Walker (11)   153
Aaron Lambley (11)   154
Adam Booth (11)   155
Wayne Davies (10)   156
Adam Duce (10)   157
Navi Challinor (10)   158
Dean Conde (10)   159
Matthew Underhill (11)   160
Claire Pinches (10)   161
Victoria Rowlands (11)   162
Matthew Jones (10)   163
William Chase-Williamson (11)   164
Hannah Williams (11)   165
Matthew Holmes (11)   166
Ashleigh Fisher (10)   167

Sir Alexander Fleming Primary School, Telford
Emma Baker (11)   168
Alex Bliss (11)   169
Antony Booth (11)   170
Paige Furnival (10)   171
Becki Hall (11)   172
Hannah McIntear (11)   173
Sophie Parker (11)   174
Declan Peate (10)   175
Tilly Perry (11)   176
Jonathan Roden (11)   177
Lucy Taffinder (11)   178
William Tinsley (11)   179
Katie Webb (11)   180
Liam Wells (10)   181

Whaley Thorns Primary School, Mansfield

The Poems

In The Sand

I was sitting in the sand,
When I thought it would be fun,
To bury my sister,
Under the boiling sun.

I started to dig a hole,
With my bucket and spade,
I dug for more than an hour,
Then I stopped to sit in the shade.

When I had finished,
I called my sister over
And told her that in the hole,
Was a four-leaf clover.

She jumped for joy
And quickly got in,
I filled up the hole,
Until it was up to her chin.

She wriggled and shouted,
I had finally got her back,
For the time when she,
Ate all of my flapjack.

Yolande Holland (11)
Bracken Lane Primary School, Retford

At The Seaside

The best part of the seaside,
Is that it's ever so wide,
After you've gone to the beach you go to the slots,
The best part is you win lots.

Another great part is the sea,
Except when you swallow it, it tastes like wee,
When I go really far out,
My mum gives me a shout!

Jamie Aaron Coggle (11)
Bracken Lane Primary School, Retford

Down By The Seaside

Driving in the car,
The seaside is not far,
My dad is on the sand,
I hit him with a band,
Oh, wow! ice cream,
This is better than a dream.

We saw the sun go by,
My sister started to cry,
We set off to play games,
I made a friend called James,
My sister ate a stick,
She was, of course, sick.

We went back to go to sleep,
It's good being at the deep,
Rebecca fell over and got a scab,
But when she did, we saw a crab,
Now it comes to the end of the day,
Except home is so far away.

Bryn Clewes (11)
Bracken Lane Primary School, Retford

The Seaside

Walking down the beach,
Trying to find shells,
Sand as white as bleach,
Donkeys ringing bells.

Dad is asleep,
Mum is sunbathing,
The sea is thigh deep,
At the ships I am gazing.

Eating fish and chips,
Sand in my eyes,
The sea is dotted with ships,
I can hear cheerful cries.

Cold Pepsi on a hot day,
Sand in the sandwiches,
Using Frisbees to play,
Sandcastles being killed by witches.

Rockpools full of starfish,
Children in the sea,
Each of them have a dream,
To catch a fish with glee.

As it starts to get dusk,
We all pile into the car,
Inside is fish and chips, a must,
We have to travel far.

The beach is almost out of view,
I had fun today!

Robert Kirk (11)
Bracken Lane Primary School, Retford

At The Seaside

The yellow sand beneath my feet,
The blue waves in the heat,
My ice cream melting in the sun,
It's crazy and the day's just begun.

My sister's buried in the sand,
All you can see is her hand,
Donkeys walking everywhere,
Oh, there's one, over there.

I go and get a bite to eat,
Fish and chips is a treat,
I go and surf in the sea,
Big waves come after me!

I go and sit in the shade
And play with my bucket and spade,
We go and walk into town,
My dad's face is a frown.

We go and play in the arcades,
To have fun as the night fades,
I wonder what I'll do next,
I'll lay on my bed and text.

I'll sit on my comfy bed
And rest, rest, rest my head,
Zzzzzzzzzzzz!
Now I'm going to sleep,
So I can count sheep.

Robyn Edwards (11)
Bracken Lane Primary School, Retford

The Seaside

Dad bought an ice cream
He held it to the sky
It started to melt
And he started to cry.

A crab nipped my toe
So I hit it back
It looked angry
So it gave me a whack!

We bought some chips
A seagull flew by
It ate my chips
I wonder why?

We were leaving
I didn't want to go now
But the tide was coming in
I wonder how?

William Abbott (10)
Bracken Lane Primary School, Retford

The Seaside

A pure white cloud drifts,
Through the endless skies,
Filled with screeching gulls
And their noisy cries.

The sea gently laps,
Against the sandy shore,
Children eat ice creams
And scream out for more.

Limpets stick their shells,
To the slimy rocks,
Gulls feast upon them,
In their many flocks.

The sun in the sky,
Shines upon the sand,
Sunlight hits the Earth
And brightens up the land.

Abigail Cooke (11)
Bracken Lane Primary School, Retford

Seaside Poems

Tides come in and out
Usually you can't walk about
When the tide comes in
You have to squeeze all the way in
Spring tides can be very dangerous
If you get stuck, you'll be famous

My dad got fish and chips
A seagull flew by
The seagull got some chips
And then the seagull said, 'Goodbye!'

My mum bought some ice cream
It was the colour of the sky
When a seagull ate it
She started to cry.

Robert Cumming (11)
Bracken Lane Primary School, Retford

What Am I?

Horrible howler
Pavement fouler
Meat scoffer
Loud cougher
Hole digger
Trouble trigger
Toiler drinker
Bathroom stinker
I'm such a hog
Do you know what I am?
I'm a . . .
Dog!

Constance Gough (10)
Braunston CE Primary School, Daventry

Throwing Up!

I threw up on a place,
I was chucked out in the rain,
My mate threw up on a boat,
It never did properly float,
My friend threw up in her dad's shoe,
She got smacked round the head, *boo hoo!*

Elizabeth Hallam (10)
Braunston CE Primary School, Daventry

The Woods In Spring

Bunnies hopping, smiling sweet,
Always eating yummy wheat,
Nibbling, munching, all the way,
Usually seen about in May.

Birds tweeting, singing high,
Normally seen in the sky,
You may see them passing by,
Love eating raspberry pie!

Badgers creeping, crawling in the night,
With another male, there might be a fight,
Digging holes deep in the ground,
Creeping up on hedgehogs, without a sound.

Rhianna Crooks (10)
Braunston CE Primary School, Daventry

Summer

S itting in the sun
U nder a tree
M eadows filled with flowers
M agpies calling others
E verything's peaceful
R esting on the grass.

James Tokley (9)
Braunston CE Primary School, Daventry

Kennings

Long thrower
Good diver
Bad fouler
Whistle blower
Good scorer
Penalty saver
Skilful player
Substitute player
Do you know what it is yet?
A footballer!

Andrew Moore (10)
Braunston CE Primary School, Daventry

Kennings

Lead puller
Meat eater
Ball catcher
Teddy savager
Rabbit chaser
Wild barker
What is it?
A dog!

Aaron Rowe (10)
Braunston CE Primary School, Daventry

Hobbits

H obits holes in the Shire
O rcs breed in Isengard
B aggins the only adventurous hobbit
B oromir killed by Urak-hai
 I sengard's army
T rolls rampage
S auron's wrath.

Sam Dawson (10)
Braunston CE Primary School, Daventry

Gymnastics

G reat fun
Y ou should come
M ats in a pile
N ew things to do
A sk for some help
S o you can do it too
T ricky
I ntelligent
C ome on in
S omersaults to do!

Molly Osborne (10)
Braunston CE Primary School, Daventry

Pitter-Patter

Pitter-patter
I'm bored at school
It's raining again
But only some drizzle.

Why can't we play
Outside in the wet?
I'd jump in some puddles
And Mum wouldn't fret.

I don't like this
Why can't we have fun?
I am *really* bored
Oh look! Here's the sun!

Annelies Tamsen Flack (10)
Braunston CE Primary School, Daventry

My Little Madam

A little madam
Doesn't go to bed
A little madam
Loves her ted

This little madam
Has a smelly nappy
This little madam
Is sometimes happy

My little madam
Counts to three
But that little madam
Really loves me.

Molly-May Allinson (10)
Braunston CE Primary School, Daventry

Summer

August . . .
No school for a month
Water fights with my brother
We are soaking wet

September
We go back to school
I play tig in the playground
Then it is home-time.

Olivia King (8)
Braunston CE Primary School, Daventry

Spiders

Ding-dong! Here comes Mr Long Legs,
Furry and creepy,
Let's hope he doesn't sleep deeply
He puts magic dust on his web
So that I walk through it
He makes me jump
When he rings the bell on his web
Then comes down on his thread.

Hannah Osborne (8)
Braunston CE Primary School, Daventry

August - Haiku

We break up from school
It is my brother's birthday
It is piping hot.

Emily Nott (8)
Braunston CE Primary School, Daventry

Slug

Slippy, slimy, horrible things
A bit like a snail
A snail has a shell on its back
A slug has nothing like that!

Bethany Snelson (8)
Braunston CE Primary School, Daventry

Family

C hris is enjoyment
H appy all the time
R unning all the time
I s funny
S ometimes silly.

Thomas Mullaney (8)
Braunston CE Primary School, Daventry

Andrew

A bsolutely lovely
N ever angry
D efinitely doesn't like a messy bedroom
R ough sometimes
E very day he is happy
W onderful!

Jessica Smith (8)
Braunston CE Primary School, Daventry

Snail Poem

What's that I see?
Some sort of shell
By the golden bell.

Hang on
There's some slime,
Some sort of crime.
Eating all my plants,
Oh no! Now there's ants!

I'm following the slime,
There's a body,
I'm getting all sobby,
Ahh! It's a snail!

Hattie Lewington (8)
Braunston CE Primary School, Daventry

Summer

September
Back to school for me
Hope I get good grades for tests
Can't wait, just can't wait!

Madeleine Gough (8)
Braunston CE Primary School, Daventry

Bumblebee

When I see a bumblebee,
I want to run free,
If you run away from them,
They sting you easily,
Their yellow and black skin scares you away from them
They are as fast as lightning
And they collect honey for their tea.

Rachel Hannah Sullivan (8)
Braunston CE Primary School, Daventry

Wasps

Flying above my head, way up high,
As fast as lightning in the sky,
They ruin the summer by flying in your dinner!
When you see their black and yellow skin,
You want to run free!
But don't confuse them with bumblebees!
You can't escape a wasp, it's hard to see,
What are you going to do,
When they corner you?

John Walvin (8)
Braunston CE Primary School, Daventry

Spider Poem

I hate spiders because they're creepy on your skin
They have to blend in
Horrible, they are rough
They have thin legs like cobwebs
You don't expect them in your dream
They have six eyes
I didn't know that
They have fangs on the bottom of their bodies.

Daisy Snelson (7)
Braunston CE Primary School, Daventry

Bumblebee Poem

Bumblebees hide in trees with a big breeze
Yellow and black, hard to clap
Which would be a harmful thing
To sting me.

Have four legs that creeps me out
It's giving me a shout
That buzzing sound that frightens me
I should run away and fast!

Ellë Osborne (8)
Braunston CE Primary School, Daventry

Wasp Poem

They make me sneeze
Because the big breeze
Zooms by.

Their sting is so painful
It makes me want to yell out loud!
In the middle of the crowd.

They are annoying like my little brother
Buzzing around me with black and yellow skin
And their bodies are like a thin pin.

Bryn Tallett (8)
Braunston CE Primary School, Daventry

Pop

D angerous because he picks up tractor weights
I t's the best going to work with him
C uts himself a lot
K eeps keys in his Shogun overnight.

Joshua Cooper (8)
Braunston CE Primary School, Daventry

Scorpion Poem

They scuttle
They creep
If you look
And peep

You will see them
Creeping up a stem

You watch out
They can kill you
What would you do?

They scare you
They can kill you
Right through!

When you go to bed
They will creep
And will peep

Poison you to death
You with have no breath!

Ashley Fisher (7)
Braunston CE Primary School, Daventry

The Seasons

Spring
Lambs leaping around
Daffodils fill the gardens
Sun peeping through clouds

Summer
Hot sun gleaming down
Holidays at the seaside
Cloudless sky above

Autumn
Conkers falling down
Walking through the crisp, brown leaves
The warm weather fading

Winter
Trudging through deep snow
Snowmen cover the gardens
Christmas on the way!

Amelia Holland (11)
Castlefields Primary School, Bridgnorth

Seasons

Spring
Spring white blossom blows
Swirling, twirling through the blue
As the sun twinkles

Summer
Summer butterflies
Drifting slowly in the air
Fluorescent colours

Autumn
Autumn cloaked in mist
Mountains covered once again
The days grow shorter

Winter
Cold winter dormice
Curled up in their bed of leaves
Waiting for the spring.

Amy-Mae Brown (10)
Castlefields Primary School, Bridgnorth

The Seasons

Spring
Calm and warm weather
Sometimes drizzling with rain
And flowers awake

Summer
The hot, golden sand
Sea glittering in the sun
And the fine weather

Autumn
The bare-looking trees
Brown leaves covering the path
Drifted from treetops

Winter
The frosty snowman
Throwing cold, frosty snowballs
Getting more frozen.

Michele Chan (10)
Castlefields Primary School, Bridgnorth

Seasons

Spring
Birds start to make noises
Leaves start to blossom on trees
Small animals are born

Summer
Sun begins to gleam
The sun reflects off objects
Sunflowers follow light

Autumn
Leaves fall to the ground
Weather starts to get colder
Apples ripening

Winter
Snow falls to the ground
Creatures' paws get stuck in snow
Everywhere is white.

Josh Savage (11)
Castlefields Primary School, Bridgnorth

Seasons

Spring
The sky, clear and cool
Summer is nearly here
Flowers, birds and warm sun

Summer
The palm trees swaying
Scorching sunlight, much too hot
Picking up some breeze

Autumn
The leaves become red
As the month changes colour
Cold breeze takes the leaves

Winter
A cold white carpet
The bleak wintry morning
Sparkling frozen streams.

Amy Corfield (10)
Castlefields Primary School, Bridgnorth

Seasons

Spring
New life has arisen
Baby lambs start to gambol
Winter tree blossoms.

Summer
The scorching hot sun
Shimmering down on the Earth
Lighting all darkness.

Autumn
Firework night is here
Dazzling colours in the sky
Watch them all explode.

Winter
Christmas time has come
Gifts under the Christmas tree
Santa has been here.

Katrina Cheshire (11)
Castlefields Primary School, Bridgnorth

Seasons

Spring
Baby lambs skipping
Beaming, golden daffodils
Flowers, birds, warm sun.

Summer
Radiant hot sun
Vivid new garden flowers
A faint buzz of bees.

Autumn
Leaves falling calmly
The first glistening frost is here
Hope of winter snow.

Winter
Snowball fights, sledging
The ground is sprinkled with snow
Dazzling, fresh winter.

Alice Wills (10)
Castlefields Primary School, Bridgnorth

Seasons

Spring
New life arrives
Flowers peep from the fine ground
April showers fall.

Summer
Blazing sun
Parasols and sandcastles
Waves upon the shore.

Autumn
Trees stand bare
Gusty winds pick up the leaves
The fire crackles.

Winter
Icy cold
Blankets of glistening snow
Are the winter's coat.

Abi Freathy (11)
Castlefields Primary School, Bridgnorth

Seasons

Spring
Buds start to open
Warm sun comes out from hiding
Spring grass emerges.

Summer
Colour everywhere
Birds call out sweet songs of joy
Summer sun rains down.

Autumn
Leaves of the autumn
Golden, crispy, magical
Falling to the ground.

Winter
Floating, falling snow
Crispy, crunchy under feet
Winter's fleece glistens.

Rebekah Mondon (11)
Castlefields Primary School, Bridgnorth

The Four Seasons

Spring
Birds pecking blossom
Baby ducklings start to swim
By dipping in a toe.

Summer
Golden sand glistens
Sunflowers turn, follow light
Swaying in the breeze.

Autumn
Golden, crispy leaves
Swirling, graceful butterflies
Leaves fall silently.

Winter
A coat of crisp frost
Covers all the trees around
It melts in the sun.

Harriet May Bratt (11)
Castlefields Primary School, Bridgnorth

The Seasons

Spring
Lambs prancing, skipping
Saffron daffodils swaying
Petals shine in the sun.

Summer
Luxurious heat
Children playing and laughing
Sweltering people.

Autumn
Golden, brown, red, green
Leaves falling and floating down
To the ground, dying.

Winter
Bitter cold, numb toes
Woolly hats and woolly scarves
Penetrating wind.

Emily Tennant (11)
Castlefields Primary School, Bridgnorth

The Seasons

Spring
Sunlight beaming down
Lambs skipping across green fields
New life appearing.

Summer
Scorching humid air
Blossom encircling the land
Sun bursting through doors.

Autumn
Leaves gold and glistening
Wind whipping and calling trees
Leaves floating to Earth.

Winter
Frost biting windows
White snow like coconut flakes
Snow carpet all around.

Cathy Slarke (11)
Castlefields Primary School, Bridgnorth

Seasons

Spring
Buds bursting on trees
Birds demolish the blossom
Wallflowers come up.

Summer
A bright light comes out
People playing on the beach
Children taste lollies.

Autumn
Crumbly leaves fall
Dark, black sky filled with patterns
Leaves change their colours.

Winter
Sparkling snowflakes fall
Ground covered in frost and ice
Warm fireplaces burn.

Amy Leanne Barber (11)
Castlefields Primary School, Bridgnorth

Seasons

Spring
New life beckons, quick!
Creatures materialise
As they come to life.

Summer
Bursting with people
Sand, golden like a medal
Piping hot sun gleams.

Autumn
Leaves blow from branches
As they fall from their safe homes
Towards a new life.

Winter
Snow falls endlessly
In unforgiving weather
Of the cold winter.

Ollie Milligan (11)
Castlefields Primary School, Bridgnorth

The Seasons

Spring
New life bounds in spring
Smells of cut grass fills the air
Trees spring back to life.

Summer
Bright light in summer
Sunflowers follow the brightness
Skylarks sing loudly.

Autumn
Bare trees in autumn
As squirrels hide their acorns
Leaves flutter to the Earth.

Winter
Harsh frosts in winter
Dead oak trees are frostbitten
Paw prints secretly lead.

Zak Chambers (11)
Castlefields Primary School, Bridgnorth

Seasons

Spring
Hibernation ends
The seeds are now being sown
The flowers are born.

Summer
The sunflowers are
Slaves to the important sun
They are disciples.

Autumn
The leaves have dropped off
The temperature has plunged
Winter is about to begin.

Winter
Snow covers the hills
Frosty ice is slippery
The air is chilly.

Ben Haddon (11)
Castlefields Primary School, Bridgnorth

Seasons

Spring
Buds spreading on plants
Birds singing loudly and swooping
Woods full of bluebells.

Summer
The boiling hot sun
Lying on the gentle sand
On beaches and boats.

Autumn
Old brown leaves falling
Fireworks lighting up the sky
Pink, orange and red.

Winter
Snow freezing the ground
Snowflakes falling and falling
Lit-up fires in homes.

Elliot Paulsen-Rakic (11)
Castlefields Primary School, Bridgnorth

Seasons

Spring
Birds tune their voices
As cloudless weather beckons
Waiting for summer.

Summer
By a cooling breeze
The summer heat is muted
As grass calmly sways.

Autumn
Swirling in the breeze
Leaves depart empty branches
Huddling on the ground.

Winter
Trees shovelled from the ground
Covered in a white blanket
Sparkling in starlight.

Jack Willett (10)
Castlefields Primary School, Bridgnorth

Rabbit-Proof Fence

Scared,
I was panicking
Dangerously
He moved us into the car
Crying

Sweating
Running wild
Scared
He was coming
Faster

Excited
Surprised we made it
Glad
Glad to be Aboriginal
Hopeful.

Matthew McLoughlin (11)
Cheswardine Primary School, Market Drayton

Hell Bay

(Based on the book 'The Sleeping Sword' by Michael Morpurgo)

This was it,
I walked out of the door,
I felt this was the right time,
The crisp smell of salt attacked my nose,
The night was cold,
I felt empty, like a ghost,
The icy wind shivered down my spine,
I felt despair,
The damp, rocky surface under my feet,
Led me on my way,
I was determined, nervous,
I could hear the raging sea,
Smashing on the cliff side,
Then I was *gone!*

Victoria Tomkinson (11)
Cheswardine Primary School, Market Drayton

The Rabbit-Proof Fence

Terrified,
I was terrified as the car flew,
Corner tilting slightly,
Melancholy,
I was traumatised,
Shoved vigorously into the car
And taken away from my family
Worried.

Gladly,
Gladly a storm started,
Worry,
I was worried the trackers would find me,
Scared.

Relieved,
I was relieved to be home,
Glad,
I was glad to see my family,
Delighted.

Sam Emmott (11)
Cheswardine Primary School, Market Drayton

Hell Bay

(Based on the book 'The Sleeping Sword' by Michael Morpurgo)

I walked over the doorstep for the last time,
I knew this was the right thing to do,
A breath of cold night air hit me in the face,
As I left the shelter of the cottage,
The sound of my bare feet slapping on the lane,
Rang out through the stillness of the night,
I tasted the salt spray on my lips,
I knew for the last time,
I felt a wave of panic sweep through me.

I took a deep breath to ease my troubled mind,
To wash away the voices that echoed in my head,
Waves of pain swept silently through my body,
As my feet stumbled up the rough track,
I climbed up, towards the brink of the cliff,
The brink of death.

I began to regret the whole idea,
But I struggled on,
Blind to what I was actually going to do,
My feet fumbled for the track,
At times, soft with springy patches of thrift
And at others, treacherous with loose rocks,
I kept on stumbling, almost giving up courage,
Then reminding myself, it's the only way out.

Over the brow of the hill, I heard the waves,
I felt the ground beneath me vibrate,
A salt-spray wind whipped my hair,
My heart began to hammer inside my chest,
I heard a clap of thunder as I took my last step,
Towards the edge of the cliff,
Towards the end of my life on Earth.

Ellenor Jane Richards (11)
Cheswardine Primary School, Market Drayton

The Trip To Hell Bay

(Based on the book 'The Sleeping Sword' by Michael Morpurgo)

The time had come,
I have to do it,
I do,
This is the way out,
Of the deep, black hole of despair.

I took my last step, out of the house,
Stumbled upon the ground,
Under me, damp salt swept thrift,
Feeling terrible,
I could hear the wind saying, 'Don't do it!'
Despair.

I felt the ground tremble violently under me,
Every step I took, I became less and less sure,
I felt the end of Hell Bay,
This was it,
The end of despair!

Charlotte Johnson (11)
Cheswardine Primary School, Market Drayton

The Trip To Hell Bay

(Based on the book 'The Sleeping Sword' by Michael Morpurgo)

One step out of my door,
Feeling confident,
I travelled up the steep, stony hill,
Felt as if I was
Just walking on into
A gloomy, black tunnel,
It never seemed to end,
The wind whistled painfully
Through my ears,
Felt the sea salt hitting my face, hard,
My heart was pounding like a loud bass drum,
I took my final step.

Kelly Watling (10)
Cheswardine Primary School, Market Drayton

Hell Bay

(Based on the book 'The Sleeping Sword' by Michael Morpurgo)

This will be the end
Of the pit of despair,
My mind was made up,
It was definite,
There I stumbled up the ragged path
Of Hell Bay,
I smelt the salted sea battering the cliff.

With my bare feet on the soft, silk thrift,
Sadness had taken over me,
I could hear the birds at their nests,
Every time a wave hit the cliff,
It was as if the ground beneath me had gone.

I reached the top of the dangerous, monstrous cliff,
I felt the power of the sea surround me,
It was though I was going to explode with unhappiness,
There I was, a gleaming ghost,
I stepped . . .

Kate Smith (10)
Cheswardine Primary School, Market Drayton

Rabbit-Proof Fence

Scared,
Have you ever been taken away?
Terrified,
I ran as fast as I could to get away,
Frightened.

Thunder,
Have you ever escaped from a place
Where you didn't want to go?
Running,
They were terrified, because they were
1200 miles from home,
Worried.

Happy,
So glad to see her mum,
Crying,
Their grandma crying
And so glad to see them,
Silence.

Amy Woodcock (10)
Cheswardine Primary School, Market Drayton

The Trip To Hell Bay

(Based on the book 'The Sleeping Sword' by Michael Morpurgo)

I peered back at my cosy house sadly,
'Sorry,' I whispered sorrowfully,
I stumbled up the road, on my scary journey,
The dark, stony, unhappy journey.

I dragged myself to the only way out,
I cried to myself, feeling sorry for myself,
I arrived,
I knew I was there,
I could smell the stinging, salty air.

No longer confident,
But I had to do it,
It's the only way out,
I was there at the end of my life,
I had to do it!
I could feel the wind on my face,
I took my last step.

Paige Wood (10)
Cheswardine Primary School, Market Drayton

The Rose Beetle Man

Ragged,
Charming, neglected, lonely,
Why is he so strange?
Rose Beetle Man has been abandoned
Like an old scarecrow,
Animals surround him in cages,
Ragged.

Lonely,
Attracts like a magnet,
Has he had any friends before?
He is so mysterious,
He can talk to recovering animals,
His eyes glow like sparkling moons,
Moves slowly around, solitary,
Lonely?

Sophie Jenkins (10)
Cheswardine Primary School, Market Drayton

Rose Beetle Man

Mysterious
Giving young animals help
Walks silently down the path
Rose Beetle Man looks like an ragged, walking shadow
Why does he carry cages?

Alister Munro (11)
Cheswardine Primary School, Market Drayton

The Rose Beetle Man

Curious
Caring, unusually scary
His hat was shapeless
His eyes are crazy and he looks very cautious
Do his eyes look weird?
Caring.

Jessica Evans (10)
Cheswardine Primary School, Market Drayton

Mystery Man

Strangely
He walks to your house and gets up to no good
His feet are full of mud
He scatters pins afar
And when you have cleaned it all up,
You shout, 'Hooray!'
Only to find it's a mess tomorrow,
So lock your door
Or get out your mop!
For the mystery man is here!

Molly Jensen (10)
Cheswardine Primary School, Market Drayton

The Rabbit-Proof Fence

Sadly,
Horribly, I was taken away by a stranger,
Nastily,
Stuck in a small, damp cage,
They stare at me,
Worried,
Happily,
I was hoping to be on my way home,
Frightened,
My sister hugging me tight,
Worried,
Tired,
Gratefully,
Her mum so happy, jumping with glee,
Sadly,
Looking for Gracie.

Emma Jones (10)
Cheswardine Primary School, Market Drayton

Colours

Yellow is the sun,
Everybody's having fun,
Green is the grass,
Waving very fast,
Black is the night,
With a lot of fright,
Red is an angry face, one that's just lost a race,
Blue is a dolphin swimming,
Wild and free in the sea.

Rebecca Bailey (10)
Edith Weston Primary School, Oakham

Olympics 2012

Lightly footed, the athlete sprints,
Gliding along the tarmac road,
One foot in front of the other, led,
Sweat runs down his burning face,
Muscles strain, tensing tight,
Training, pumping, feet tapping light,
The red, white, blue vest bulges with expression,
The sun beating down on his tiring body,
He stops and gazes, puffing hard,
Tired, he trudges to the land of nod.

Dreaming that he'll some day be
The owner of a medal on the podium, yes he,
All cameras approach him, the winning athlete,
He smiles at his mother, who stands in pride,
Noises from the crowd a distant hum,
His National Anthem rings out through Britain.

Now he stands, heart pounding like thunder,
He is the athlete with the right commitment,
Years of waiting, now he's here,
The gun awaits his faithful fear,
He stretches as the crowd dies down,
He's trained; he's ready now to compete,
He sprints as the bullet rushes into thin air,
The finishing line his friend,
The competitors the enemy,
He pants, he strains, he gives all his energy,
The end creeping up on him,
Awaiting the winner . . .
No one knew this British lad
Could be capable of stealing the medal on the podium stand.

Grace Hodge (11)
Edith Weston Primary School, Oakham

A Treacherous Horse Fight

A shadow appears in Tyson's field,
A newcomer has arrived,
I will tell you of a treacherous fight,
He's lucky that he survived.

They stand half a metre apart,
Waiting for the other to run,
Tyson charges and knocks her down,
The newcomer screams like she was shot by a gun.

The newcomer rises with blood on her back,
Turns around and kicks Tyson's head,
Tyson falls and faints on the ground,
The opponent thinks he's dead!

The newcomer rears up with joy
And neighs out into the air,
Then she gallops around and gallops away,
Tyson lifts his head to stare.

He clumsily gets up onto his feet
And moves very stiffly away,
He is shaken by this treacherous fight,
As he walks from the place where he lay.

Rosie Pitts (11)
Edith Weston Primary School, Oakham

What Am I?

Cute, tiny eyes,
What a shame, me and my family quickly dies,
Little wiggling gills,
Have amazing swimming skills,
A massive munch, crunch,
Delicious, I'm a shark's lunch,
I'm a loving pet,
That's always wet,
When I wake up in the pond,
It's good to see the sun has dawned,
We have blunt teeth
And still live in the coral reef,
On top of the cupboard in my tank at night,
It's scary because we're afraid of the height,
Sometimes, when I'm shy,
It's good to look up at the beautiful sky,
We may have weak bones,
But still jump over sea cones,
Oh yummy, fish food,
It really tastes so good,
My delicate feathered fins,
Work just like birds flying wings,
Small, gleaming tails,
Shiny, golden scales,
What am I?

A goldfish!

Keiran Carty (11)
Edith Weston Primary School, Oakham

Darkness

When Mum tells me to go to bed,
I stamp my feet and shake my head.
But before I know it, I'm in my room,
The only light, the new full moon.
She flicks off my switch and closes my door,
I start to miss her more and more.
The light fades fast, the shadows appear,
Here comes the darkness, I start to fear.
It crawls over the walls, so quiet and quick,
I start to feel really sick.
It's scary, so I curl up in my bed.
But even when I pull the covers over my head,
Plain black is all I can see -
It is creeping up on me.
That's it! I can't take this anymore,
So Mum comes up and opens my door!

Jessica Whight (11)
Edith Weston Primary School, Oakham

Teachers At Night!

Have you ever wondered
What do teachers go to sleep in?
PJs or a nightie?
Well, let's go and see.

There's Mrs Brown,
Heavily breathing (snoring)
Sleeping in her nightgown
And where's Mrs Mais?
Under the covers I see
Dozing in her PJs.
What about Mr Firt?
Tossing and turning a lot
Dreaming away in just a T-shirt.
Where's Mrs Fee?
She's not on the bed I see
Oh, she's under it in her pink nightie
And there's Mr Fare,
With his thumb in his mouth
Only in his underwear!
What about Mr Pyranna
He's calling for his teddy
In his one-piece pyjamas.
So after all that
We have found out
That teachers wear normal things in bed
Like pyjamas, underwear and T-shirts
Just like *us!*

Katie Jones (11)
Edith Weston Primary School, Oakham

I Remember Jack

He stands on cliffs, eagle-eyed and sentry
Clean, protecting, shining through the mist,
Only bright light bulbs are on his list
Through the dark, the rain, day and night,
Jack soon works, shiny bright,
His sound, his roar,
Will keep you off the rocky shore
Ghosts of past ships, go sailing by,
Who never heeded old Jack's cry
Jack never smiles, never sleeps,
Stand tall, protecting all,
Two tonnes of pain to dress him well,
To keep all seamen from going to deep sea's Hell,
Old, lonely Sam tends to Jack's needs,
Keeps him smart and free of weeds,
Old Sam has died and Jack shines no more,
No brightness, no sound,
Poor Jack has been smashed to the ground.

Ainsley Flanagan (11)
Edith Weston Primary School, Oakham

The Writer Of This Poem

(Based on 'The Writer Of This Poem' by Roger McGough)

The writer of this poem . . .
Is as small as a mouse
As slow as a snail
As strong as a house.

Daniel Edge (9)
Ellesmere Primary School, Ellesmere

The Writer Of This Poem

(Based on 'The Writer Of This Poem' by Roger McGough)

The writer of this poem . . .
Is taller than a tree
As artistic as a paint brush
As noisy as can be.

As giggly as a baby
As silly as a chimp
As silly as a joke
And it makes me limp.

Rebecca Gilman (8)
Ellesmere Primary School, Ellesmere

The Writer Of This Poem

(Based on 'The Writer Of This Poem' by Roger McGough)

The writer of this poem . . .
Is taller than a tree
As brave as a lion
And as musical as a bee.

As creative as a mad scientist
As happy as a smiley face
As clever as a super computer
And as fast as a race.

Jac Roberts (8)
Ellesmere Primary School, Ellesmere

The Writer Of This Poem

(Based on 'The Writer Of This Poem' by Roger McGough)

The writer of this poem . . .
Is taller than a high rise flat
As fast as an athlete
As ugly as a rat

As sporty as a cricket bat
As funny as a joker
As bouncy as a bunny
As silly as a smoker

The writer of this poem . . .
I hope is not a bloke
She is not a million, billion
Hope she can take a joke.

Alana Hall (9)
Ellesmere Primary School, Ellesmere

The Writer Of This Poem

(Based on 'The Writer Of This Poem' by Roger McGough)

The writer of this poem . . .
Is braver than a hound
As sporty as a footballer
As funny as a clown.

Josie Butler (8)
Ellesmere Primary School, Ellesmere

The Writer Of This Poem

(Based on 'The Writer Of This Poem' by Roger McGough)

The writer of this poem . . .
Is taller than a tree
As sporty as a footballer
Is stronger than a flea.

Jordan Evans (8)
Ellesmere Primary School, Ellesmere

The Writer Of This Poem

(Based on 'The Writer Of This Poem' by Roger McGough)

The writer of this poem . . .
Is smarter than a smoothie
As mathematical as a sign
As creative as a sharp pencil

As tall as a tree
As musical as a bee
As strong as a knee
As mathematical as me.

George Carsley (8)
Ellesmere Primary School, Ellesmere

The Writer Of This Poem

(Based on 'The Writer Of This Poem' by Roger McGough)

The writer of this poem . . .
Is taller than a house
As sporty as a tennis ball
As creepy as a mouse

As musical as a flute
As funny as a clown
As dramatic as a stage
As grumpy as a frown.

Chloe Molloy (9)
Ellesmere Primary School, Ellesmere

The Writer Of This Poem

(Based on 'The Writer Of This Poem' by Roger McGough)

The writer of this poem . . .
Is faster than a jumbo jet
As elegant as a gliding flamingo
As helpful as a welcoming vet

As sporty as a polished cricket ball
As mature as cheddar
As lively as a springing lamb
And I'll never be a liar, forever!

As nutty as a fruit cake
As funny as Peter Kay
As clever as Miss Marple
And when something is impossible, he'll find a way.

The writer of this poem . . .
Is always your man
As mathematical as an add sign
Now he's going in his van.

Sam Todd (9)
Ellesmere Primary School, Ellesmere

The Writer Of This Poem

(Based on 'The Writer Of This Poem' by Roger McGough)

The writer of this poem . . .
Is as funny as a clown
As chubby as a gorilla
As happy as an upside-down frown

As strong as an arch
As mature as cheese
As tall as a church
As lively as an army of bumblebees

As talented as a gymnast
As helpful as a lollipop lady
As artistic as a paint brush
As musical as Slim Shady

The writer of this poem . . .
Is a bit of a dope
He's one in a million, billion
I hope he can take a joke.

Liam Jones (9)
Ellesmere Primary School, Ellesmere

The Writer Of This Poem

(Based on 'The Writer Of This Poem' by Roger McGough)

The writer of this poem . . .
Is taller than a pyramid
As silly as a monkey
As crazy as a frog.

Bradley Llewellyn (8)
Ellesmere Primary School, Ellesmere

The Writer Of This Poem

(Based on 'The Writer Of This Poem' by Roger McGough)

The writer of this poem . . .
Is taller than a house
As silly as a chimpanzee
And ticklish as a baby.

Shannon Bate (9)
Ellesmere Primary School, Ellesmere

The Writer Of This Poem

(Based on 'The Writer Of This Poem' by Roger McGough)

The writer of this poem . . .
Is taller than a skyscraper
As clever as a calculator
As thin as paper

As active as a chimpanzee
As funny as Peter Kay
As demented as a chicken
Who likes to lie on the bay

As musical as a drum
As fast as a bolt of lightning
As arty as can be
The most frightening person ever to be seen

As sporty as a cricket bat
Just been whacked in the tooth
I hope the reader of this poem
Knows it's not the truth!

Scott Demmerling (9)
Ellesmere Primary School, Ellesmere

The Writer Of This Poem

(Based on 'The Writer Of This Poem' by Roger McGough)

The writer of this poem . . .
Is taller than a tree
As forgetful as a rock
As arty as can be

As funny as a clown
As sneaky as a fox
As mucky as a pup
As clumsy as a box

The writer of this poem . . .
Never gets through a maze
She's one in a billion
That's what people say!

Ffion Davies (9)
Ellesmere Primary School, Ellesmere

The Writer Of This Poem

(Based on 'The Writer Of This Poem' by Roger McGough)

The writer of this poem . . .
Is as mucky as a pup
As tall as a giraffe
As woolly as a tup

As arty as a Smartie
As giggly as a baby
As friendly as a VIP.

Hannah Green (9)
Ellesmere Primary School, Ellesmere

The Writer Of This Poem

(Based on 'The Writer Of This Poem' by Roger McGough)

The writer of this poem . . .
Is as intelligent as a book
As crazy as a cow
As daring as a cook

As ecstatic as a balloon
As scruffy as a tramp
As sad as a ghost at his lowest gloom
Like girls at Brownie camp

As smiley as a clown
As cute as a kitten
As boring as a noun
As soft as a mitten

As fast as a jockey
As wooden as a puppet
Like boys playing hockey
As mad as a muppet!

Kathryn Leggett (9)
Ellesmere Primary School, Ellesmere

The Writer Of This Poem

(Based on 'The Writer Of This Poem' by Roger McGough)

The writer of this poem . . .
Is as crazy as a frog
As mad as a bear
As mad as a dog

As cool as a cat
As funny as a pup
As boring as a mat
As hard as a stump

As weird as a fly
As brave as a fox
As sad as a pie
As boring as a box

As caring as a teddy
As fat as a bear
As hyper as Freddy
As good as a fair

As lazy as a rabbit
As stupid as a rock
As weird as a hobbit
As cool as a lock.

Connor Jones (9)
Ellesmere Primary School, Ellesmere

The Writer Of This Poem

(Based on 'The Writer Of This Poem' by Roger McGough)

The writer of this poem . . .
Is as happy as a frog
As crazy as my mum
As tall as a tree

As kind as a bent banana
As crazy as a lad
As shiny as a suit of armour
As crazy as a dad

As naughty as a baby boy
As kind as a mouse
As small as a pup.

Joe Griffiths (9)
Ellesmere Primary School, Ellesmere

The Writer

(Based on 'The Writer Of This Poem' by Roger McGough)

The writer of this poem . . .
Is as wise as a tawny owl
As naughty as a hyper puppy
As quiet as a tiger's prowl

As honest as a fairy's wish
As noisy as a lion's roar
As sporty as a swimming fish
As strong as a wild boar

The writer of this poem . . .
Is good at mostly all
Except for keepy uppies
He's not very good with a ball!

He's as fast as the cheetah's miles
As jumpy as a jumping bean
As snappy as some crocodiles
But isn't always clean!

The writer of this poem . . .
Isn't just like that
He can do other things as well
He can hang upside-down like a bat!

Nicholas Stokes (9)
Ellesmere Primary School, Ellesmere

You!

You!
Your head is like a bowling ball
You!
Your ears are like battered potatoes
You!
Your eyes are like rocks
You!
Your nostrils are like tennis rackets
You!
Your mouth is like a lump of grass
You!
Your hands are like rotten sticks
You!
Your belly is like a giant bowl
You!
Your legs are like metal bars
You!
Your backside is like a bouncy ball.

Joe Hall (9)
Ellesmere Primary School, Ellesmere

Best Friends

Best friends are kind-hearted,
Best friends make you laugh,
Best friends have belief in you,
Best friends are good fun.

Best friends are good-natured,
Best friends play and care,
Best friends laugh at jokes,
Best friends are always there.

Best friends are always honest,
Best friends are pleased to help,
Best friends can't help joking,
Laugh, I cannot help!

Emily Digby (9)
Ellesmere Primary School, Ellesmere

Bedtime Killer - Kennings

Fun waggler
Eye blinker
Shark killer
Rock scraper
Fish eater
Water drinker
Quick swimmer
Mysterious creature
Eye peerer
Fast thinker
Clumsy creature
Bedtime killer.

Liam Robert James Gittins (10)
Ellesmere Primary School, Ellesmere

The Bible

The Bible is the best
Not all of you agree

The Bible is the best
Why don't you care at all?

The Bible is the best
Just try your best

The Bible is the best
Please look after it properly.

Jordan Minor (8)
Ellesmere Primary School, Ellesmere

The Land Of Mermaid Moo

In the land of Mermaid Moo
The sharks and dolphins go *boo!*
They show off their bums
And have lots of fun
They obviously don't have a clue.

In the land of Mermaid Moo
The sea-phin goes tu-wit, tu-woo,
They look like fairies,
But they are very hairy,
They should belong in a zoo!

In the land of Mermaid Moo,
Octopuses have the flu
Except for one
Who explodes like a bomb,
His name is Bubbly Blue.

Oh, the Mermaid Moo! The Mermaid Moo!
That's the place for me and you!
So chop-chop, let's stride,
The bus leaves at half-past five
For the land of Mermaid Moo!
The excellent Mermaid Moo, Moo, Moo!
The amazing Mermaid Moo!

Emily Lloyd (10)
Ellesmere Primary School, Ellesmere

Rainbow Jigsaw Fish - Haikus

Rainbow jigsaw fish
Carefully gliding creature
Amber coloured face.

Dangerous, light fins,
Ocean gleaming, sapphire-blue
Gliding like a bird.

Long, thin, stick-like legs
Sharp tail, flickers like the fire
Colour explosion.

A vibrant body
Gently tearing the ocean
Rainbow jigsaw fish.

Jessica Price (11)
Ellesmere Primary School, Ellesmere

The Mysterious Wonder

They are the kings of the sea,
As smooth as a pearl,
Its echoes can burst your ears.

An emerald glow in its eye,
It flies through the sea,
The nature of a dolphin.

The killer whale's pattern,
As quick as a shark,
A mysterious wonder.

Its echoes flow through the waves,
It whines like a whale,
Warning creatures in its path.

It owns the grace of a swan,
As loud as a bear,
The dominance of lions.

This creature is not common,
But is friendly so,
Let's treat the Whalesphin as we know.

Jessie Thea Owen (10)
Ellesmere Primary School, Ellesmere

Pink Spiker - Kennings

Yellow shimmer
Fast swimmer
Pink spiker
Water liker
Pot belly
Moves like jelly
Fish eater
Shark treater
Sea creeper
Big weeper
Slow slider
Gentle glider.

Lauren Edge (11)
Ellesmere Primary School, Ellesmere

Dolphin

Dolphin, dolphin, gliding through the sea,
Looking for fish, for his tea,
Ever so   quiet,
            quiet,
            quiet.

Some careless clownfish swims right on -
Chew, chew, swallow, gone!

Now having had a full meal,
He passes a group of seals
And jumps right out of the blue.

Hannah Lewis (9)
Ellesmere Primary School, Ellesmere

Stingpus - Cinquain

Gliding
Like an eagle
Through the colourful waves
A moving sunset in the deep
Gliding.

Matthew Jasper (10)
Ellesmere Primary School, Ellesmere

Rainbow Butterfly Fish - Haikus

Rainbow butterfly
Swaying through the blue ocean
Rainbow butterfly

Vibrant coloured fish
A rainbow in the blue sea
Pink fluttering wings.

Jessica Amy Rogers (11)
Ellesmere Primary School, Ellesmere

The Diamond Of The Deep - Cinquains

Slinking
Roams leisurely
Fluorescently cruises
Undulating purposefully
Perfect

Vibrant
Glistening tail
Burst of colour explodes
Graceful beauty presents its path
Always!

Fiona MacKellar (11)
Ellesmere Primary School, Ellesmere

Feet Chocker - Kennings

Fast swimmer
Loves dinner
Leg locker
Feet chocker
Shark biter
Fat fighter
House keeper
Sea creeper
Big beater
Gigantic leaper!

Kenny Griffiths (10)
Ellesmere Primary School, Ellesmere

Inside The Creature's Tummy

Inside the creature's tummy,
There are things that are very funny,
Such as trolleys and swings
And many other things,
He also eats runny honey!

Inside the creature's tummy,
Where the food is very runny,
The water is sour
And reeks of flour,
So the creature cries, 'Mummy, Mummy!'

Inside the creature's tummy,
Where the food is very scrummy,
The meat is raw,
So he breaks the law
And the bread in prison is crummy!

Oh, the creature's tummy! The creature's tummy!
That's the place for my boring mummy!
So run, run away!
You might be there one day
For the creature's tummy
Is not a place to be
The creature's horrible tummy!

Patrick Gilman (11)
Ellesmere Primary School, Ellesmere

My Fish - Cinquain

Flipping
Like a dolphin
Happy as a petal
Like a flower in the ocean
Flipping.

Catrin Warner (11)
Ellesmere Primary School, Ellesmere

Crab-Ray

The electric crab,
Couldn't lay down a slab.

The very strange fish,
Doesn't use a dish.

The sea danger,
Isn't a stranger.

The instant crash,
Wouldn't ever smash.

It's a crab-ray!

Gregory Dyke (10)
Ellesmere Primary School, Ellesmere

Toucan - Cinquain

Slowly
Walking slowly
Tall and colourful too
Flying through the sky and rushing
Slowly.

Harriet Beau Klapproth (9)
Ellesmere Primary School, Ellesmere

In The Land Of Octo-Sands

In the land of Octo-Sands
Ariel claps her hands
The catfish spies the dog
One fish looks like a hog
Its prey is weird, but also cool
Not forgetting grand!

In the land of Octo-Sands
Seaphin has pink hair strands
The starfish is stung by jelly
And now is nicknamed Ellie
Who plays in the upcoming bands!

In the land of Octo-Sands
Fish swim the lands
The shark causes a commotion
And walks in an angry motion
As now he has learnt to stand.

Oh, the Octo-Sands, the Octo-Sands
It really is quite grand
So hurry, let's run!
The train leaves at one
For the land of Octo-Sands
The wonderful Octo-Sands, Sands, Sands
The wonderful *Octo-Sands!*

Bethany Davies (10)
Ellesmere Primary School, Ellesmere

The Land Of Sea-Phin Bay

In the land of Sea-Phin Bay,
I have nothing to say,
But looking at the fishes,
Carrying their own dishes,
Who speak to me every day.

In the land of Sea-Phin Bay,
I always have some delay,
When I go to the zoo
And go to the loo,
I never have time to play.

In the land of Sea-Phin Bay,
Everyone says, 'OK,'
I don't know why,
But they always lie
And swim in a weird way.

Oh, the Sea-Phin Bay,
Let's get there straight away,
So hurry! Let's run!
The train's leaving at one,
For the land of Sea-Phin Bay,
The wonderful Sea-Phin Bay, Bay, Bay,
The wonderful Sea-Phin Bay!

Beth Cooter (10)
Ellesmere Primary School, Ellesmere

Fat Head - Kennings

Slow swimmer
Orange shimmer
Ginormous nose
Mouldy toes
Jelly belly
Watches telly
Claw scratcher
Shark catcher
Dolphin eater
Fish beater
Eyes red
Fat head.

William Hughes (11)
Ellesmere Primary School, Ellesmere

My Dog

My dog is really mad
He acts like a hyena
He eats off the floor

He loves walkies
He jumps up at anyone
He likes food too much

He eats the sofa
He can be really funny
He is my best friend!

Alexander Davies (9)
Ellesmere Primary School, Ellesmere

Monkey Troubles - Haikus

Monkeys swing from trees
They are normally cheeky
They like bananas

They have light brown fur
And hands and feet just like us
With big and small toes

There are lots of types
Like orange orang-utans
And spider monkeys

They have curly tails
They also live in the zoo
Just the crazy ones

They have cheeky grins
And teeth as sharp as needles
But still not as fierce

Monkeys are naughty
They live in greeny jungles
Also they're cunning

Their eyes glow at night
They shine brightly in the sun
Must go out and play.

Caithlin Williams (9)
Ellesmere Primary School, Ellesmere

Cat Power - Haikus

As soft as velvet
Eyes like glimmering diamonds
Ginger as the sun

Cats are very cute
Cats prowl around at midnight
Cats are cool and great

Claws, spiky as pins
Their noses wet as the rain
Tongues red as blossoms

Cats fight in the dark
Cats creep up to catch their prey
And love everyone.

Leanne Jones (8)
Ellesmere Primary School, Ellesmere

My Dog Chad - Haikus

Chad is my pet dog
Chad is a grey scruffy dog
Chad used to be white

Sleeps in a basket
Likes to eat dog food for tea
A cute, cuddly dog

Curls up in his bed
Lots of warm, cuddly blankets
Has a blue basket.

Isobel Lloyd (8)
Ellesmere Primary School, Ellesmere

Gemstone - Haiku

Gemstones glisten and
Gemstones gleam in the light all
Shimmering clean - cool!

Bonnie Jackson (9)
Ellesmere Primary School, Ellesmere

My Funny Little Dog - Haiku

Roll a ball and I
Will catch it, roll me over
And tickle my tum.

Louise Challinor, Alastair Scott & Bradley Maltby (9)
Ellesmere Primary School, Ellesmere

Snake - Haiku

You spring at your prey
And slither across the ground
Like a speedy worm.

Jake Saunders (9)
Ellesmere Primary School, Ellesmere

About A Cat - Haiku

You sleep by the fire
All cosy, warm and curled up
Like a ball of fluff.

Jessica Jones (9)
Ellesmere Primary School, Ellesmere

About A Rabbit - Haiku

You are so fluffy
I love your soft fur so much
You eat the flowers.

Chloe Jones (9)
Ellesmere Primary School, Ellesmere

About A Cat - Haiku

You are so fluffy
When you sleep you purr quiet
Sometimes you're dirty.

Sophie Tearle (9)
Ellesmere Primary School, Ellesmere

About A Monkey - Haiku

Oh, what a cheeky
Monkey, eating bananas
And dropping the skins.

Georgette Klapproth (8)
Ellesmere Primary School, Ellesmere

My Dog - Haiku

You are so fluffy
You are like a soft, feather
Pillow, I love you.

Charlie Austin (9)
Ellesmere Primary School, Ellesmere

The Guinea Pig - Haikus

Rusty, you are small
Running round your cage at night
You squeak and you bite

Rusty, the fluff ball
Your teeth are like little twigs
Rusty's nice to me.

Aaron Jones (8)
Ellesmere Primary School, Ellesmere

Underwater - Haikus

Pacing silently
A lonesome blade, all bloodstained
Scared, alone, abused

No light in its heart
Once a dark, murderous wreck
Now a floating grave.

Ellie Johnson (9)
Ellesmere Primary School, Ellesmere

Haikus

Sharp, dagger-like teeth
Monstrous legs, they move slyly
Fluorescent fish fins

Whipping tentacle
As strong as a suction pipe
Fluorescent fish fins

Strong, rubber-like sword
Evil, threatening eyes dart
Sharkafrogastomp!

Lucy Hill (11)
Ellesmere Primary School, Ellesmere

You!

You!
Your nose is as long as a snake
You!

You!
You're as mean as a rhino
You!

You!
Your bottom smells like a pongy drain
You!

You!
Your belly is like a bouncy ball
You!

You!
You're as fast as a cheetah
You!

You!
Your tail is as long as a flame
You!

You!
Your mouth is like a little worm
You!

You!
Your hair is as long as a giraffe
You!

You!
Your head is as wobbly as a jelly
You!

You!
Your skin is as rough as tarmac
You!

You!
Better leave or else
You'll get a spook.

Abigail Lear (10)
Ellesmere Primary School, Ellesmere

You!

You!
Your bottom is like a lump of dough
You!
Your nose is as long as a snake's body
You!
Your eyes reflect the beautiful moonlight
You!
Your tusks are like sword pockets
You!
Your nose is like a kids' play slide
You!
Your mouth is like the smile of a donkey
You!
Your tail is like a filthy mop
You!
Your legs are like tree trunks
You!
Your eyes are like blue sapphires
You!
Your belly is like a big, round football
You!
Your bum is like a crystal maze
You!
You're scared of little white mice
You!
Your feet are like big volcanoes.

Hollie Cottam (10)
Ellesmere Primary School, Ellesmere

Tiger Trouble - Haikus

They have burning bright
Eyes that light up in the night
See prey any day

Trotting away is
Fast paws and very sharp claws
Stealing life away

All camouflaged fur
Hiding in the night for prey
He will strike for life

Tiger face the night
Not even wanting to fight
Looking through the trees.

Florence Whittle (9)
Ellesmere Primary School, Ellesmere

Copycat - Haikus

I'm a copycat
Copying is a fun game
Copy is my name

Copy me, copy
Even copy bumblebee
I'm copying you!

Meg Parkinson (8)
Ellesmere Primary School, Ellesmere

Our Teacher

Our teacher is rotten
Her face looks like a dog's bottom
That's why she's forgotten
How to sew with cotton.

Emily Slack (9)
Ellesmere Primary School, Ellesmere

Fragers

F ear inflictors
R ace destroyers
A lways hidden
G reat killers
E xtra power
R ocket speed
S uper boom!

Be careful around these fish
Because they are highly deadly
And will go *boom!*

Tom Moore (10)
Ellesmere Primary School, Ellesmere

Environment

E is for enjoyable places, going everywhere
And having fun
N is for nature, stop killing wildlife
And put your litter in the bin
V is for visiting zoos and seeing all the different animals in cages
And using animals in circuses
I is for incredible creatures doing anything they are told to
By their masters or keepers in zoos
R is for rubbish meaning leaving the litter on the floor
Which may harm the animals
O is for the octopus swimming
In the deep blue sea
N is for the Nile crocodile
Swimming in the water
M is for mammals being hunted by humans
For their fur
E is for energy
Coming from the sun
N is for nutritious plants
That you get from the soil
T is for tigers being slaughtered by man
And kept for food.

Amy Bowers (10)
Hadnall CE Primary School, Shrewsbury

Survival

E is for elephant being grey and muddy
N is for narwhal with his sharp horn
V is for viper spitting deadly venom
I is for impala jumping in danger
R is for rock python sliding on the rocks
O is for octopus with its long arms
N is for newt sliding in the seaweed
M is for manta ray gliding in the water
E is for electric eel shocking everyone
N is for Nile crocodile prowling in the water
T is for tiger lurking in the bushes.

Ellie Davenport (9)
Hadnall CE Primary School, Shrewsbury

Animals

Animals in the universe killed every day
By litter, pollution and rubbish thrown away
Junkyard mayhem making animals ill
Destroying habitats on the side of a hill
Black and white cows munching on grass
Turned into a hamburger on a plate of brass
The wildebeest gets killed for merchandise and gold
Then suddenly taken away and sold.

Beth Davies (10)
Hadnall CE Primary School, Shrewsbury

The Environment

The ice in the Antarctic melts because of global warming
Caused by the acts of humans.

The litter covering the Earth from the top to the bottom
Humans could help by recycling the rubbish.

There are problems with bird flu
Caused by human carelessness.

So in all, humans are the problems with our Earth
But what should we do?

Elliot Fox (11)
Hadnall CE Primary School, Shrewsbury

Blue Whale

This endangered mammal whistles in the sea
Bigger than a human, larger than a tree
The extraordinary mammal is dying out
It blows water out of its spout
The whale's skin feels like leather
The whalers stay out hunting, no matter the weather
This massive creature is giant in size
Next to its plates are its eyes
Remember, keep the whales going
Then you might see one when you're rowing.

George Watkin (9)
Hadnall CE Primary School, Shrewsbury

Pollution

Pollution is a harmful thing
Like an invisible thick cloud
Which is giving a painful sting

Although we don't know it
We are killing our planet
It will soon be the end of the world

Litter is clogging
Litter is foul
We are doing it
So let's stop it now

So really, let's stop it
This awful thing
And let the world sing!

Ellie Deer (11)
Hadnall CE Primary School, Shrewsbury

Run

I went back in time,
To buy a rhyme,
From the dinosaur land.

I came home in time,
With my rhyme
And noticed it was a dinosaur head instead,
Run!

I went forward in time,
To buy a rhyme,
From the future land.

I came home in time,
With my rhyme
And noticed it was pollution instead,
Help!

I went back in time,
To buy a rhyme,
But bought a dinosaur head.

I went forward in time,
To buy a rhyme,
But bought some pollution instead.

Amy Roberts (11)
Hadnall CE Primary School, Shrewsbury

The Prince Of The Ocean

Shark, shark, weaving in the ocean
Trying to kill its prey
As itself, it is in danger from man and pollution
Shark, shark, weaving in the ocean
It is dangerous for the others
Some could be known as its brothers
But only other sharks
They're the princes of the ocean.

Tait Johnson (9)
Hadnall CE Primary School, Shrewsbury

Environment

E is for eagles soaring up high
N is for narwhal swimming in the deep
V is for voles scurrying through the grass
I is for impala galloping through the fields
R is for rats running through the sewers
O is for owl flying silently after a mouse
N is for nature as a whole
M is for mackerel gliding through the water
E is for eel lying in the mud
N is for nightingales singing a sweet chorus
T is for tiger hunting in the trees.

Lauren Forwood (9)
Hadnall CE Primary School, Shrewsbury

The Scorpions

S corpions are dangerous and poisonous creatures
   That have a very big sting on the end of their tails
C laws that kill their enemies
O pen claws that help it defend itself
R eady to kill prey
P oisonous stings that paralyse its prey
I t is a very dangerous creature
O f course, it can hurt you very badly
N ot a good house pet
S mall but very dangerous creatures.

Kenny Nixon-Herron (10)
Hadnall CE Primary School, Shrewsbury

Pollution

Pollution runs through the town,
Up, down and all around,
On the towers, in the streets
Down below in a heap
On the ground, rubbish fills in the gutters,
Where is spills
Water runs in streams that flow
Down the rocky hill it goes
Kids who play in muddy parks
Don't know the chemicals that can harm.

Rebecca Parry (9)
Hadnall CE Primary School, Shrewsbury

Litter Is Bad

L itter is deadly and a killer
I s this why animals keep dying?
T he birds nest inside crisp packets and suffocate
T he litter is bad for wildlife and animals
E ven though the bin is far away
R emember to put litter in the bin!

Tom Willett (8)
Hadnall CE Primary School, Shrewsbury

The Bird

As the bird swoops in the air
It dodges the other birds
It moves as swiftly as a fox
The bird jolts and turns in the other direction
Suddenly the bird sees something on the ground
The bird swoops down
At high speed
Down goes the bird
He gets his head stuck in a glass bottle
The bird is down without a fight.

Jordan Deer (10)
Hadnall CE Primary School, Shrewsbury

Pollution Invades

It stalks like a killer
Killing all in its path
Once done it can't be reversed
Birds, plants and humans
None can survive it
With clouds of grey
Smoke invades
Killing the sky and the sun
Acid rain comes every day
The weather is always the same
Only one thing can do all this
This is . . .
Pollution!

Tyler Holland (10)
Hadnall CE Primary School, Shrewsbury

Litter

The leaves are blowing from side to side
The litter is whirling in the wind
An ant scurries by
Its long, thin body and six legs moving
Like it had just been hit by lightning
The ant goes for food
But is disturbed by incoming rubbish
As the sun rises
Warming the Earth
The ant returns to its habitat
The ant comes out for a rest
And is trapped inside a package
Even a small ant is affected by our rubbish
Dumped by humans.

George Dillon-Jones (11)
Hadnall CE Primary School, Shrewsbury

The Dolphin

Dolphins, dolphins
Jumping in the sea
It's a wonderful, beautiful sight
Both for you and me
Dolphins, dolphins
Communicating with each other
Who are they talking to?
It could be their brother
Dolphins, dolphins
Racing in the ocean
Swimming after little fish
And catching in slow motion.

Luke Williams (9)
Hadnall CE Primary School, Shrewsbury

The Frog

Tadpoles are so small
Except when they're older
They change into frogs

When they're older
They jump so high!
They spring into the air

When they're older
They're so big
Eyes are brown

Skin is slithery
Hands with three fingers
Tadpoles have tails, but frogs don't.

Conor Johnson (9)
Hadnall CE Primary School, Shrewsbury

Epitaphs

Here lies the body
Of Bugs Bunny
He got killed
By a carrot in his tummy

Here lies the body
Of Winnie the Pooh
His head was flushed
Down the loo!

Here lies the body
Of Scooby Doo
He got killed
When a cow went *moo!*

Charlie Warren (8)
Ordsall Primary School, Retford

Epitaphs

Here lies the body
Of Rhys Dolby
He got pushed in a bush
And went all mouldy.

Here lies the body
Of Kyle Taylor
He got run over
By a boat and a sailor.

Here lies the body
Of Sam Wright
She got stabbed to death
By an old, ratty kite.

Megan Lyth (8)
Ordsall Primary School, Retford

Epitaphs

Here lies the body
Of old Miss Chad
Sending all the children
Crazy and mad.

Here lies the body
Of crazy Miss Ward
Chopped to death
By an electric cord.

Here lies the body
Of mad Mrs Mann
Got hit on the head
With a frying pan.

Here lies the body
Of lazy Mr Rust
Choked to death
On a piece of dust.

Joanna Allman (9)
Ordsall Primary School, Retford

Shots Day

Doctors love the day
When the needles are delivered!
They jump,
They laugh,
Waiting
For the
Patients to
Start rolling
In. Shots
They're called,
For disease
And to draw
Blood for a
Test. Unwrap
The package
Hold patient's
Arm, slide
Through
Skin
Push
Down
Ow!

Kestra Walker (11)
Pontesbury CE Primary School, Shrewsbury

The Little Classroom Of Horrors!

At the crack of dawn,
The moon fixes her glaring eyes,
On the little classroom
A riot of noise begins!
The snapping trays have been woken,
Now they're waiting hungrily for human flesh,
To wander into their gaping mouths
The noise has awoken the arrogant wind chimes
Soon they start babbling about their wealth and good looks
Next, the lazy computer moans and groans furiously
Thinking about the horrible children in the morning
His nightmares have disturbed the worst of them all
The sinister OHP
He is not hesitant on staring psychotically
While plotting a destructive revenge!
Dawn is fast approaching
And the little classroom of horrors
Is sweetly falling asleep
Waiting patiently . . .
For their next *victims!*

Aaron Lambley (11)
Pontesbury CE Primary School, Shrewsbury

Humpty Dumpty Takes Up Sport!

Humpty Dumpty tried to play cricket,
Not very wise to stand behind the wicket!

Crack!

Humpty Dumpty tried to play rugby,
A lot worse happened than just getting muddy!

Crack!

Humpty Dumpty tried to play rounders,
Didn't play by the rules - upset the founders!

Crack!

Humpty Dumpty after three *bonks* on the head,
He's taking up cooking instead!

Adam Booth (11)
Pontesbury CE Primary School, Shrewsbury

Scary Classroom Poem

I saw a pile of books fall without a touch,
I felt a breeze, but the window wasn't open,
I smelt something rotten in the air,
I heard people talking, but there wasn't anybody there,
I touched the door handle and it disappeared,
I discovered a computer gone,
I came across the laptop, flickering on and off.

Wayne Davies (10)
Pontesbury CE Primary School, Shrewsbury

The Football Fans

The crowd roars as the footie players walk onto the pitch
When the whistle goes, all is silent,
When the home team score, the away fans get violent,
Final whistle gone, empty places in the away fans' seats,
While the home fans chant, sing and dance.

Adam Duce (10)
Pontesbury CE Primary School, Shrewsbury

December

D is for drops of snow, snow to play in
E is for excellent presents, the best all year
C is for Christmas, everyone's favourite day
E is for Eve, Christmas Eve when Santa comes out to play
M is for mountains all covered in snow
B is for biscuits, for Mr Claus to eat in delight
E is for everlasting dinner, with pork, broccoli, potatoes and carrots
R is for Rudolph, carrots for him, see you next year!

Navi Challinor (10)
Pontesbury CE Primary School, Shrewsbury

Sisters

Can't get in the bathroom,
Really need a wee,
Ella's looking in the mirror,
Always doing her hair.

Can't get to the toilet,
Really need a wee,
Amy's looking in the mirror,
Always doing her face.

Ella and Amy out of the bathroom
Just about to have my wee,
Then Mum barges past,
Oh no! Time's run out . . .

Dean Conde (10)
Pontesbury CE Primary School, Shrewsbury

Jungle Fun

Racing through the jungle,
Swinging on the trees,
Acting like a monkey,
Doing as I please!

I am the strong one,
The king of the jungle,
If you ever see me,
I'd run for your life!

Rifling through the jungle,
Doing what I want,
I'm always gonna catch you,
When I'm on the run,
Having jungle fun!

Matthew Underhill (11)
Pontesbury CE Primary School, Shrewsbury

The Seaside

It sounds like birds singing in the summer
Flying and eating, that's them!
It tastes like dead fish,
That have been caught by fishermen,
The sea looks blue and green,
With dark yellow sand,
The seaside.

The waves are roaring
And getting angry,
White horses on the tips of waves,
The waves are trying to eat me!
The seaside.

The tide's crawling in
Quicker and quicker it crawls
The waves surrounding me,
Eating and grinding their teeth
Like an evil monster
Help! I'm being eaten!
The seaside.

Claire Pinches (10)
Pontesbury CE Primary School, Shrewsbury

Never Forever

Love is sweet,
Also kind,
Sometimes nice
And it's always on my mind.

But if you,
Let it go,
Your life will seem,
Oh, so slow.

So keep it near,
In your heart,
You can put up a fight,
For your loving sweetheart.

So now you've caught it,
In your heart,
You can go off racing,
In a horse and cart.

But before you go,
You have to know,
It's gonna end soon,
So take it slow!

Victoria Rowlands (11)
Pontesbury CE Primary School, Shrewsbury

The Miracle Of Life

A long time ago
In a dark, scary wood,
An egg lay there,
Like a rugby ball,
Just standing there,
Under a tree.

Suddenly, it cracked,
Like the miracle of life,
The dragon spat fire
And singed some wood.

Now a dragon was born
And it was the miracle of life.

Matthew Jones (10)
Pontesbury CE Primary School, Shrewsbury

Love

I walked in the room,
How lovely she was,
Tip-toed closer,
How beautiful she was,
Doing her hair,
How pretty she was,
Talked to me
And how I wish she were mine!

William Chase-Williamson (11)
Pontesbury CE Primary School, Shrewsbury

I'm Sorry

I'm sorry to cry,
I'm sorry for sorrow,
Will this pain ever stop?
I was thinking about you all day!
But you weren't thinking about me,
Were you?
I haven't stopped,
No, not yet,
I'm thinking about it though,
What are you up to?
Oh, just text me back,
Because my heart's about to crack!

Hannah Williams (11)
Pontesbury CE Primary School, Shrewsbury

It's Holiday Time

We're going on holiday today
Everyone's getting packed
We're going to France
To see all the beautiful places
And the amazing views

We're going on holiday today
And I'm really excited
We are going on a plane
Soaring high above the clouds

We're going on holiday today
To the sea and the sandy beaches
Everyone is so happy
Looking forward to a vacation
I just know that we are going to have a brilliant time!

Matthew Holmes (11)
Pontesbury CE Primary School, Shrewsbury

Birthdays

B is for bouncy castles
I is for icing, the best bit of the cake
R is for the ripping sound as I open my presents
T is for the tiredness when all my friends are gone
H is for the happy people enjoying the party
D is for the dog, my best birthday present
A is for the apple bobbing, my favourite party game
Y is for the yearly fun I have
S is for the shouting of the *Happy Birthday* song

The best birthday ever!

Ashleigh Fisher (10)
Pontesbury CE Primary School, Shrewsbury

A View From My Bedroom Window

Looking out of my bedroom window,
I see dim lights, hidden behind rows and rows of houses,
The light from the lamp posts
Let off bright orange light,
That shines on the soaked road,
The oil on the footpath causes a shiny rainbow
To appear in the blackness.

Cats screech as people walk past,
One by one, two by two, the people walk by,
Motorbikes zoom by noisily, like a mass of stags,
The dogs bark loudly next door,
As a search helicopter flies above.

I hear a drip and then a drop,
As murky water plops onto the porch roof,
The shadows of the trees are frightening
Like spirits floating freely,
A flock of birds fly, swiftly
And then, the night is dead . . .

Emma Baker (11)
Sir Alexander Fleming Primary School, Telford

A View From My Bedroom Window

Out of my bedroom window I can see:
A big tree rustling in the wind,
A big garden with four nice big trees,
Cars whooshing by, with their lights nice and bright,
I can see the fields blowing in the wind
And sometimes, there's a tractor coming down
Also the birds going in and out the rooftops
And walking around scaring me,
I can see the bulging bright light over the road, at the pub,
The music from the pub going on too late at night,
My dog snoring and growling his head off, in his dreams,
The sky, on a clear night, seeing the moon shining like silver,
Twinkling stars glittering brightly,
The planes in the sky, flashing like shiny stars,
With their tail lights flickering on and off, red and blue,
Stars and planes getting mixed up, thinking they're one and the other,
Animals running around like they're in a game,
Having lots of fun, but they're not.

Alex Bliss (11)
Sir Alexander Fleming Primary School, Telford

Through My Window After Dark

The trees look tall
Dancing in the dark
People looking tired
After work lights
Are flickering off
And on through the night

The moon looks bright
In the night the stars
Look like a disco
Ball shining in
The dark.

Antony Booth (11)
Sir Alexander Fleming Primary School, Telford

Through My Window After Dark

As I look out my bedroom window
I see people walking around,
Cars driving around,
Headlights off the cars, searching.

The moon is shining,
The sky dark and black,
The stars glittering in the sky
And all of them looking beautiful.

Paige Furnival (10)
Sir Alexander Fleming Primary School, Telford

A View From My Bedroom Window

Looking into the gloomy night, I see,
Lights flickering on and off, like fireflies,
Moon and stars twinkling like glitter,
Lamp posts in the distance like stars shining.

People walking, their footsteps crunching,
Crackling,
Dogs barking, growling.

I hear people shouting, arguing,
The cars are wild animals, growling, snarling,
A branch hits my window, scratching, scraping.

The rain gently drips, splashing down the pipe,
Cats miaowing, screeching, screaming,
My little brother, snoring, gently, gently.

Becki Hall (11)
Sir Alexander Fleming Primary School, Telford

A View From My Bedroom Window

The neighbourhood is not very lively,
Not many people are awake,
The street light glows faintly,
Like the moon up above.

Scary shadows move across the windows,
One star and the moon,
Has to brighten the night sky,
My garden is very dark,
Nothing to see at all.

The dark sky,
Like the dog with the man,
Big, black shadows walk by,
Suddenly,
It is quiet once more,
Peaceful,
Everything is still.

Hannah McIntear (11)
Sir Alexander Fleming Primary School, Telford

A View From My Bedroom Window

A clear night and the trees blowing,
The misty air outside,
All the people talking,
Cats miaowing at the back door,
A bright lamp,
What is it?
A street lamp, of course!

Looking out at the midnight-blue,
All sparkling stars,
Cars shuffling by,
One
And then another.

Seeing a quiet street,
Silent,
Bright moonlight shining through the window,
The moon as clear as could be.

Neighbours cooking, clinking saucepans,
Eating,
Calmly going to bed,
Sleeping,
My reflection showing through the window,
Goodnight . . .

Sophie Parker (11)
Sir Alexander Fleming Primary School, Telford

Through My Window After Dark

As I look out of my bedroom window
I see the glittery stars
The trees rustling in the wind
One lone star twinkling
People walking down the street

Garage doors banging
Cars going up and down the road
House lights going on and off
And the moon making the top of a tree light up
Lamp posts making the branches light up.

Declan Peate (10)
Sir Alexander Fleming Primary School, Telford

A View From My Bedroom Window

I see the trees blowing,
As the night draws in,
Street lamps glow,
As the cars return home.
I hear the dog barking
At the cats,
As they are chasing the little black bats
Hear the bins, crashing, *crash, crash!*
Car alarms go *bleep, bleep,* like grasshoppers in the grass
The ladybirds sing in the drainpipes.

Hear the leaves flying by,
Look at the stars in the sky,
Like a frog in a pond,
With a big, long tongue.

Tilly Perry (11)
Sir Alexander Fleming Primary School, Telford

A View From My Bedroom Window

A clear night and the dogs are barking,
The front door slams like someone's angry,
A bright light from a street lamp,
The area is quiet,
I hear people talking,
Quietly in the darkness.

I hear a helicopter going past,
My neighbour's cat is miaowing to get in the house,
Looking out of my window at midnight black
I hear buses go by
One
And then another.

I see people in the window, eating their dinner,
Bright moonlight shining through the window,
Calmly going to bed,
Sleepy.

Jonathan Roden (11)
Sir Alexander Fleming Primary School, Telford

A View From My Bedroom Window

It is quiet and the lamp flickers on and off
Cars come by every five minutes
One after another
Faint noises of dogs barking in the distance
The wind blows quietly and moves
Near the night.

Feet go *clip-clop*
Handbags and purses go *clitter-clatter*
Faint noises of gates closing
The night is finally here
As I look up to the sky
I see the moon shining bright
Stars glitter above me
As the wind blows by, the trees go *swish, swoosh*
Wet leaves jump on my window.

As I open my window
The smell of wet leaves crowds my nose
Like a nose clip that will never come off
As I look at the frost
A doughnut ring comes out
And slides down the icy hill
Like a man covered in butter sliding down a slippery slide.

As I look down below
I see frost covering my cars and garden
I can see my mum, pulling up onto the drive
The night is near an end.

Lucy Taffinder (11)
Sir Alexander Fleming Primary School, Telford

A View From My Bedroom Window

From my window I can see:
Cars going past one by one, roaring like dragons
And the darkness of the night floating
Like an alien ship with starry lights
I hear the wind whistling by, like birds
The swing is a mini skyscraper with birds as planes.

Sometimes it is silent
As if everything were gone
But then I hear a dog barking like a fierce dinosaur
My fence is like a dark barrier
Keeping out the people who walk up and down
Like drums being battered, *pitter-patter*
I hear a bell as my cat trots across the garage
Like a tiger in the wild.

The moon is like a cheerful face
But then disappears into a blanket of clouds
The frosty ground crunches as my dad puts his fishing stuff back
Jingle, jingle goes the bell on the dog's collar
As its owner takes it for a walk in the frosty night
I smell fresh air as if my window is open
And the frosty window ledge is white and cold
The breeze brushes against my face
And cools the heat down from my radiator.

William Tinsley (11)
Sir Alexander Fleming Primary School, Telford

A View From My Bedroom Window

From my room I can see . . .

A gloomy night with no stars
My brother's motorbike sitting on the road
There are lovely plants blanketing the grass
A baby screams loudly next door
There are people walking on by
And light of my school like
The light of the lamp post in front of my house
There is a car revving to get warm
In the freezing cold air.

There are trees with leaves
But branches neatly breaking
On the pavement of every drive
There are some cars
All freezing cold
The houses all over my street with lights on
But not next door, they've gone away
There is a sound of my cat miaowing
In the garden at next door's dog
My other next door neighbour is unloading things
From his dirty, red van.

It's getting dark
Cars begin to fade
No cars or people are going by.

My street is lonely
I can't hear much
But across the road,
Silent people get in their car to go home
From visiting friends or relatives.

Katie Webb (11)
Sir Alexander Fleming Primary School, Telford

Through My Window After Dark

As I looked outside my window
I saw and heard a dog barking,
I heard mini motors going down the street, revving engines,
People coming home from work with chips,
The wind whistling when wafting the leaves off trees.

As I look up at the sky
I see the moon, it looks like a cake,
I see stars sparkling,
Dark shapes of a shed and trees,
Garage doors slamming,
Cats fighting on the wall.

Liam Wells (10)
Sir Alexander Fleming Primary School, Telford

A View From My Bedroom Window

The rumble of bins as they get put out,
Feet going *crunch, crunch*
On the cold frost of the clear night,
Dark, big and scary,
The house stands tall, black
And for hours the lights are one,
The clear sky with the moonlight,
Hard soil road,
Cars chasing like a cat with a mouse,
Then four garages squeaking open,
All the nine cars go,
In a dark sleep, like a kitten in a box,
Gardens covered with frost,
The moon shines and the stars help her
Brighten the sky.

Ami Currell (10)
Sir Alexander Fleming Primary School, Telford

Through My Window After Dark

As I looked out of my bedroom window
I saw cats fighting, people being dragged down the street
Walking their dogs,
Then it's all quiet, then a car's headlights
Like a blinding beam appeared out of nowhere
And people coming home from work,
The moon is dull and round and lights up the sky
The stars twinkle in the sky like a sparkly necklace
The sky is orange when the moon goes down
The sky is as black as coal that goes on forever.

Josh Doyle (11)
Sir Alexander Fleming Primary School, Telford

World War II

There are tanks and Spitfires
And loads of vehicles that make fire
Watch towers, loads of them everywhere
Night watchers, wolves, German army
English army, all different armies
The tiger, a tank, a real-life tank
Gas masks you wear when smoke comes
Hitler's Germany's leader.

Cory Arrowsmith (8)
Whaley Thorns Primary School, Mansfield

Dragons And Fairies

There once was a dragon all big and strong,
He didn't brush his teeth and his feet did pong,
One day a fairy went by singing,
'I'm going to make blueberry pie, blueberry pie, oh yes I am!'

The fairy saw the dragon, 'What's your name?'
'My name is Smauge the big, bad pain!'
'My name is Moonlight,
Please don't give me a fright,
I'm only a sprite!'
'I'm going to eat you, sprite and I'm quite all right!'
Moonlight tapped his nose, Smauge arose
And sang, brushed his teeth and cleaned his feet and said,
'I'm having grass, not the sprite.
'Want a tea party?'
'Yes.'

Faye Bennett Newbury (8)
Whaley Thorns Primary School, Mansfield

My Best Friend, Shannon

My best friend is Shannon,
She really is a help when I am by myself in the playground,
She goes and asks me if I want to play with her,
She sits next to me at dinner time
She's my bestest, best friend,
She really is the best, best friend ever!

Chloe Eva Langley (9)
Whaley Thorns Primary School, Mansfield

Football

Football rocks, it's the best
Come on and play it and bring your friends
It never ends.

Bang! Whizz! Fireworks go off when you never know
Come on and let's go today
Go and watch Manchester United
See them beat West Ham
Come and get a ticket, now £75.00 for one.

All of us like to watch football
Buy a football, play football
Join a team and play.

Jake Knight (9)
Whaley Thorns Primary School, Mansfield

The Sunset

T he sunset is hot
H ave a lovely sun tan
E very day it is hot

S un, sun, sun
U sually hot
N ever cold
S it in the sun
E very day it is hot
T ry to wear summer clothes.

Chelsea Marie Bull (10)
Whaley Thorns Primary School, Mansfield

England Crazy

England crazy,
England mad,
I support England
And I am very glad,
We will, we will, beat you,
We will, we will, beat you,
Meat pie, sausage roll,
Come on England, score a goal!

Adam Parsons (10)
Whaley Thorns Primary School, Mansfield

Revolting Monster

There is a noise downstairs,
It sounds like lions and bears,
It's giving me the scares,
I creep down the stairs,
I open the door,
Argh!
There stood a revolting monster,
As tall as you could see,
It's mouth all crumbly,
It's belly all rumbly
And it's coming after *me!*

Bethany Evans (9)
Whaley Thorns Primary School, Mansfield

Art

Glitter or glue, you can draw a shoe,
Paint or colour, you know what to do,
Just mess about, don't go out and shout.

Just do art!

You can draw people, pots and pans
And if it was a club, you'd have lots of fans,
You can have art in colour, or black and white,
But the best thing about it is, it can't give you a fright!

Rebecca Gilding (10)
Whaley Thorns Primary School, Mansfield

Football Crazy

F ootball's good, football's mint
O h and I'll give you a little hint
O n the pitch having a match
T heir goalie can't catch
B all's coming towards me
A nd I try to pass to Lee
L oads of games to go
L et's start the Premiership and let it flow

C onnor's got the ball
R un on, their team's too small
A nd Connor passes to Ray
Z ego tries to tackle the ball
Y ou know what he does, he scores!

Charlie Smith (9)
Whaley Thorns Primary School, Mansfield

Happiness

It sounds like laughter in the streets
It tastes like chips, gravy and meat
It smells like water in a pool
It looks like my friend, she is cool
It feels like the fluffiest dog around
It reminds me of the shell I found.

Louise Vincent (11)
Whaley Thorns Primary School, Mansfield

Happiness

It sounds like people playing
It tastes like fresh bread
It smells like freshly-cut grass
It looks like ducks flying south
It feels like the softest dog in the world
It reminds me of my friends laughing.

Holly Limb (11)
Whaley Thorns Primary School, Mansfield

Happiness

It sounds like laughter in the playground
Where children are making a very loud sound
It tastes like sausage and chips with potato ships
It smells like flowers near the big towers
It looks like the shining sun, with a bun
It feels like jelly in my belly
It reminds me of my mamma makin' when we're having fun!

Katie Carrington (11)
Whaley Thorns Primary School, Mansfield

Happiness

It sounds like children's laughter during playtime
It tastes like a double chocolate chip muffin melting in my mouth
It smells like Skegness water at sunrise
It looks like a newborn lamb wakening
It feels like being loved for the first time
It reminds me of waves crashing up against Ibiza rocks.

Jasmin Holmes (10)
Whaley Thorns Primary School, Mansfield

Happiness

It sounds like children laughing and having fun
It tastes like bacon sandwiches with tomato ketchup
It smells like freshly-cut grass
It looks like the moonlight, shining down on the water
It feels like a hug from my mum
It reminds me of me and my family together walking along the beach
While me and my little brother paddle in the sea.

Adam Booth (10)
Whaley Thorns Primary School, Mansfield

Happiness

It sounds like a drum banging
It tastes like melted cheese on toast
It smells like raw eggs
It looks like an old tree
It feels like jelly
It reminds me of a Springer spaniel.

Kyle Scott (10)
Whaley Thorns Primary School, Mansfield

Happiness

It sounds like a fairground
It tastes like vanilla whipped ice cream
It smells like chocolate sauce
It looks like drips of rain
It feels like a cold winter's day
It reminds me of ice cream on a day last week.

Evangeline Comins (11)
Whaley Thorns Primary School, Mansfield

Happiness

It sounds like waves of the tide coming in
It tastes like the most delicious chocolate cake in the world
It smells like the sweetness of a flower
It looks like the beautiful colours of a rainbow
It feels like the silk of a beautiful butterfly's wings
It reminds me of the sun beginning to rise for a brand new day.

Victoria Booker (11)
Whaley Thorns Primary School, Mansfield

Love

It sounds like children having fun
It tastes like a big Sunday roast
It smells like fresh air
It looks like a big, red love heart
It feels like a gust of wind
It reminds me of a hot summer's day.

Chelsea Lauren Rodgers (11)
Whaley Thorns Primary School, Mansfield

Sadness

It sounds like children screaming
It tastes like old smelly bread
It smells like gone-off cheese
It looks like someone being crucified
It feels like jumping on a hard bed
It reminds me of old milk.

Samuel Evans (11)
Whaley Thorns Primary School, Mansfield

Sadness

It sounds like a lightning bolt striking from the sky
It tastes like a piece of mouldy bread
That has been left outside for two years
It smells like a piece of mouldy cheese
It looks like a strike of lightning
It feels like an arrow hitting your heart
It reminds me of a small child crying in the morning.

Scott Robinson (11)
Whaley Thorns Primary School, Mansfield

Happiness

It sounds like children's laughter on the beach
It tastes like Galaxy that melts in my mouth
It smells like water from the sea
It looks like the stars shining in the sky
It feels like the softest silk lace
It reminds me of going to Cumbria and seeing the sunset
On the deep blue sea in summer and winter.

Bethany Livingstone (10)
Whaley Thorns Primary School, Mansfield

Happiness

It sounds like children screaming in the playground
It tastes like crispy cheese and tomato pizza with red sauce
It smells like hot sausage rolls
It looks like a new school book
It reminds me of my dad's Simpsons cushion.

Ricky Bolton (10)
Whaley Thorns Primary School, Mansfield

Happiness

It sounds like a circus
It tastes like chocolate cake
It smells like ice cream
It looks like an alligator
It feels like a feather
It reminds me of my dad.

Tom Holland (11)
Whaley Thorns Primary School, Mansfield

Happiness

It sounds like children in the playground
It tastes like crispy bacon with tomato sauce
It smells like eggy bread
It looks like sunlight shining on the water
It feels like my mum and dad and brother
It reminds me and my mum and dad and brother
At the seaside, at Skegness.

Denise Vickers (11)
Whaley Thorns Primary School, Mansfield

Sadness

It sounds like children crying
It tastes like a rotten egg
It smells like soggy bread
It looks like children drawing
It feels like wet trousers
It reminds me of my friends crying.

Paige Wakeling (10)
Whaley Thorns Primary School, Mansfield